гоck

potatoes

potatoes

Great recipe ideas with a classic ingredient

Marshall Cavendish
Cuisine

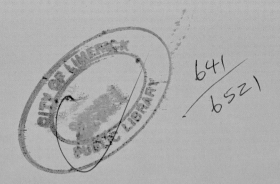

The publisher wishes to thank Lim's Arts and Living, and Sia Huat Pte Ltd for the loan and use of their tableware.

Design: Tan Shiang Chin
Photography: Jambu Studio

Copyright © 2005 Marshall Cavendish International (Asia) Private Limited

Published by Marshall Cavendish Cuisine
An imprint of Marshall Cavendish International
1 New Industrial Road, Singapore 536196

Other Marshall Cavendish Offices
Marshall Cavendish Ltd. 119 Wardour Street, London W1F 0UW, UK • Marshall Cavendish Corporation. 99 White Plains Road, Tarrytown NY 10591-9001, USA • Marshall Cavendish International (Thailand) Co Ltd. 253 Asoke, 12th Flr, Sukhumvit 21 Road, Klongtoey Nua, Wattana, Bangkok 10110, Thailand • Marshall Cavendish (Malaysia) Sdn Bhd, Times Subang, Lot 46, Subang Hi-Tech Industrial Park, Batu Tiga, 40000 Shah Alam, Selangor Darul Ehsan, Malaysia

Marshall Cavendish is a trademark of Times Publishing Limited

National Library Board Singapore Cataloguing in Publication Data
Potatoes in 60 ways. – Singapore : Marshall Cavendish Cuisine, c2005.
p. cm.
ISBN : 981-261-221-1
1.Cookery (Potatoes) I. Title: Potatoes in sixty ways
TX803.P8
641.6521 -- dc21   SLS2005047779

Printed in Singapore by Times Graphic Pte Ltd

contents >>

introduction >>

Available in abundance and at a relatively low cost, potatoes are one of the most versatile foods available today. This is illustrated in the myriad ways the humble tuber is transformed into tasty dishes ranging from soups and salads to pies and casseroles, in the recipes here.

Potatoes are a rich source of nutrients, containing minerals, vitamins B and C as well as 2 percent protein. As most of the nutrients lie just beneath their skins, it is advisable to cook and eat potatoes unpeeled, unless otherwise specified in the recipes. To cook potatoes in their jackets, gently scrub and wash well before use. Where peeling is preferred, use a vegetable peeler to keep the peelings as thin as possible.

Regardless of variety, always look for potatoes that are smooth, firm and fairly clean when making your purchase. Steer clear of potatoes with wrinkled or wilted skins, cut or bruised surfaces, soft dark areas and discolouration. Potatoes with green patches or sprouting should also be avoided as they contain a mildly toxic compound called solanine, which may lead to illness when consumed. Finally, keep away from potatoes with a musty or mouldy smell as this may be an indication of decay.

Potatoes should be stored in a cool, dry, dark and well-ventilated place since high temperatures and exposure to sunlight encourage the growth of green patches and sprouting. Do not wash potatoes before storing as dampness increases the likelihood of decay. Store separately from strong-smelling fruits and vegetables, for example, onions, as potatoes absorb odours easily, hence affecting their flavour. Generally, potatoes with high starch and low moisture levels can be kept for up to several weeks if stored properly. Potatoes which contain a lot of moisture and very little starch are best consumed within a few days of purchase as they are likely to decay faster.

The wide variety of potatoes available commercially today is generally classified according to skin colour, shape, size and use. Major varieties available include russet, white, yellow, purple, baby and red potatoes. Apart from determining how perishable potatoes are, the amount of starch and moisture in potatoes also determine the texture of potatoes when cooked, and therefore the most suitable cooking methods.

Potatoes with high levels of starch and little moisture contain starch granules which absorb internal moisture, then expand and burst as the potatoes cook. This results in a floury texture when these potatoes are boiled, or a dry, fluffy texture when baked. Potatoes with medium starch and moisture contents are considered as all-purpose potatoes suitable for most kinds of potato dishes. Potatoes with low starch and high moisture levels have a firm, waxy texture when cooked. They are suitable for preparations such as boiling, roasting and steaming, where the potato pieces are required to hold their shape through the cooking process.

Potato Varieties and Cooking Methods

The potato varieties listed here are by no means exhaustive, given the hundreds of types of potatoes available today. The potatoes used in this book are also of the more common varieties available to make sourcing of the ingredients easier.

Russet Potatoes

These large, dusty-coloured potatoes are one of the most common varieties available commercially. With their high starch and low moisture levels, russet potatoes are extremely popular for making into French fries that are crisp on the outside and fluffy on the inside, as well as baked potatoes. Russet potatoes are also highly suitable for mashing and puréeing as they achieve a floury texture when boiled. The floury texture also allows mashed russet potatoes to bind well with other flours to be made into breads and a type of Italian potato pasta called gnocchi.

White and Yellow Potatoes

White and yellow potatoes have thin, smooth and pale-coloured skins. These potatoes have medium starch and moisture levels, and are therefore known as all-purpose potatoes. Long white potatoes are oblong-shaped potatoes with a medium starch level, suitable for pan-frying, mashing, baking, steaming and roasting. Some all-purpose yellow potatoes include the Yukon Gold—potatoes which possess yellow flesh and a rich flavour, and the Yellow Finn potatoes, yellow-fleshed potatoes known for their buttery and creamy texture.

Purple Potatoes

Purple potatoes have smooth, purple-coloured skins, and flesh that ranges from purple to white colour. With their medium starch level, purple potatoes are all-purpose potatoes which have a nutty flavour and add an interesting colour to mashed potato, salads and French fries.

Baby Potatoes

Baby potatoes, also known as new potatoes, are small potatoes with flaky, paper-thin skins. They contain little starch and a lot of moisture, which gives rise to their smooth, creamy texture when cooked. Baby potatoes are popular as they can be cooked and served whole. These potatoes are extremely suitable for steaming, roasting and boiling. Due to their very high moisture content, baby potatoes are more perishable than other potatoes and should be consumed within a few days of purchase.

Red Potatoes

Red potatoes have smooth red skins and pale yellow flesh. These potatoes contain very little starch and a lot of moisture, which result in their firm and waxy texture when cooked. As red potatoes hold their shape well after cooking, they are great for preparing salads and casseroles, dishes which require the boiling of potatoes.

salads

japanese potato salad

This refreshing salad has a delicious dressing, comprising Japanese rice wine vinegar, olive oil and mayonnaise.

Serves 4

Ingredients

Russet potatoes	450 g (1 lb)
Japanese rice wine vinegar	2 tsp
Olive oil	1 tsp
Salt	$\frac{1}{2}$ tsp
Japanese cucumber	1, halved lengthways, seeded and thinly sliced
Brown onion	$\frac{1}{2}$, peeled and thinly sliced
Ham	3 slices, cut into thin strips
Mayonnaise	4 Tbsp

Method

- Put potatoes into a pot of boiling salted water. Return to the boil, reduce heat and simmer for 15–20 minutes or until tender. Drain, peel and mash.

- When potatoes are still hot, add rice wine vinegar, olive oil and salt. Mix well. Leave aside to cool.

- Mix mashed potatoes, cucumber, onion and ham together with mayonnaise.

- Refrigerate to chill for an hour before serving. Garnish as desired.

potato and radish crunch

A fresh tasting salad perfect for a lovely picnic.

Serves 4

Ingredients

Potatoes	450 g (1lb)
Butter	50 g (2 oz)
White bread	3 thick slices, crusts removed and cut into 1-cm ($^1/_2$-in) cubes
Cucumber	5-cm ($2^1/_2$-in) piece, cubed
Red radishes	6, thinly sliced
Dry roasted peanuts	25 g (1 oz)
Chives	1 bunch, snipped
Salt	to taste
Ground black pepper	to taste
Sour cream	4 Tbsp

Method

- Put potatoes into a pot of boiling salted water. Return to the boil, reduce heat and simmer for 15–20 minutes or until tender. Drain well. When cool, cut into 1-cm ($^1/_2$-in) cubes.

- Melt butter in a frying pan. When sizzling, add diced bread and fry gently until golden. Drain well. Set aside to cool completely.

- Combine potato cubes, fried croutons, cucumber, radishes, peanuts and chives in a salad bowl. Season with salt and pepper to taste. Add sour cream and mix gently before serving.

NOTE

Watch the potatoes carefully: they should be cooked through but still firm. If overcooked, they will break up and be difficult to cut into neat cubes. Mix gently so that the ingredients are thoroughly coated in the sour cream but remain separate.

potato and prawn salad

This is an easy to prepare salad with the contrasting textures of creamy potatoes, eggs and crunchy prawns.

Serves 4

Ingredients

Potatoes	450 g (1 lb)
Mayonnaise	3 Tbsp
Dried tarragon	3 Tbsp
Salt	to taste
Ground black pepper	to taste
Eggs	2, hard-boiled, shelled and chopped
Prawns	100 g (3½ oz), cooked, peeled and chopped
Cucumber	1, sliced
Chives	1 small bunch, snipped

Method

- Put potatoes into a pot of boiling salted water. Return to the boil, reduce heat and simmer for 15–20 minutes or until tender.

- Drain, peel and chop potatoes roughly. Mix with mayonnaise, tarragon, salt and pepper to taste. Leave to cool for about 1 hour.

- When cool, mix potatoes with chopped eggs and prawns. Spoon into a deep serving dish. Serve with sliced cucumber and garnish with snipped chives.

potato and capsicum salad

This tasty salad is a great accompaniment to grilled or barbecued meats.

Serves 4–6

Ingredients

Baby potatoes	450 g (1 lb), scrubbed
Green capsicum (bell pepper)	1
Celery	2 stalks, diced
Onion	1, peeled and finely chopped
Cucumber	1/2, peeled and diced

Dressing

Sour cream	150 ml (5 fl oz / 10 Tbsp)
French mustard	1 tsp
Cayenne pepper	a pinch
Salt	1 tsp

Method

- Put potatoes into a pot of boiling salted water. Return to the boil, reduce heat and simmer for 15–20 minutes or until tender. Drain and leave to cool completely.

- Remove pith and seeds from capsicum. Slice a small section finely and set aside for garnish. Cut remainder into small cubes.

- Combine capsicum cubes, celery, onion and cucumber together in a salad bowl.

- Cut potatoes in half and mix with vegetables. Cover and refrigerate until required.

- Just before serving, make dressing. Combine sour cream in a bowl with mustard, cayenne pepper and salt. Mix well. Pour dressing over salad and toss together.

- Garnish with sliced capsicum and serve immediately.

NOTE

Use American mustard instead of French mustard for a milder flavour.

Add 100 g (3 1/2 oz) chopped ham to make this salad more substantial as a meal.

gado gado
(indonesian salad)

This is an Indonesian salad of potato slices and cooked vegetables served with a rich peanut sauce.

Serves 4

Ingredients

Potatoes	2, boiled and sliced
Cabbage	¼, shredded and steamed
Water convolvulus (*kangkong*)	100 g (3½ oz), steamed
Bean sprouts	100 g (3½ oz), scalded
Firm bean curd	2, deep-fried and sliced into 1 x 2-cm (½ x 1-in) pieces
Cucumber	½, sliced into rounds
Eggs	2, hard-boiled, shelled and sliced into rounds
Fried prawn crackers	

Sauce

Fresh red chillies	8
Dried prawn paste (*belacan*)	1 tsp
Cooking oil	2 Tbsp
Shallots	8, peeled and finely sliced or 1 brown onion, peeled and finely sliced
Coconut milk	375 ml (12 fl oz / 1½ cups)
Peanuts	70 g (2½ oz), roasted and coarsely crushed or 125 g (4½ oz) crunchy peanut butter
Palm sugar (*gula Melaka*) or brown sugar	1–2 tsp
Tamarind juice (*See note*)	60 ml (2 fl oz / ¼ cup) or 30 ml (1 fl oz / 2 Tbsp) lemon juice mixed with 30 ml (1 fl oz / 2 Tbsp) water
Salt	to taste

Method

- Pound chillies and dried prawn paste together until a fine paste is achieved.

- Heat oil and sauté shallots or onion gently until soft. Add ground mixture and stir-fry for 4–5 minutes.

- Add coconut milk, a little at a time, then add all other ingredients for sauce. Simmer for about 3 minutes until sauce thickens. Set aside to cool to room temperature.

- Arrange salad ingredients in a deep serving dish. Just before serving, pour sauce over and toss lightly. Garnish with fried prawn crackers.

NOTE

The vegetables in this recipe should be lightly cooked so that they remain crisp. To make tamarind juice, soak 1 Tbsp tamarind pulp in 60 ml (2 fl oz / ¼ cup) warm water for 5 minutes. Squeeze pulp with fingers, then strain to remove any fibre and seeds.

warm sausage and potato salad

Potatoes and sausages smothered in a creamy tarragon and chive dressing.

Serves 4

Ingredients

Baby potatoes	700 g, unpeeled, scrubbed and halved
Sausages	8–10, cut into 4-cm (2-in) lengths
Onion	½, peeled and finely chopped
Mayonnaise	3 Tbsp
Sour cream	150 ml (5 fl oz / ½ cup)
Paprika	2 tsp
Dried tarragon	1 Tbsp
Chives	1 bunch, cut into short lengths
Ground black pepper	to taste
Salt	to taste

Method

- Put potatoes into a pot of boiling salted water. Return to the boil, reduce heat and simmer for 15–20 minutes or until tender.

- Leave potatoes in pot with water. Add sausages to warm them through. Cover and set aside.

- To make dressing, mix together onion, mayonnaise, sour cream, paprika, tarragon and chives. Reserve some chives for garnish. Season with salt and pepper to taste.

- Drain potatoes and sausages well. Toss gently with dressing and transfer into a deep serving dish. Sprinkle with reserved chives and serve warm.

belgian warm salad

This is a hearty potato salad with a wine vinaigrette dressing.

Serves 4–6

Ingredients

Potatoes	350 g (12 oz)
French beans	350 g (12 oz)
Butter	25 g (1 oz)
Streaky bacon	225 g (8 oz), cut into fine strips
Spanish onion	1, peeled and finely chopped
White wine vinegar	60 ml (2 fl oz / 4 Tbsp)
Salt	to taste
Ground black pepper	to taste

Method

- Put potatoes into a pot of boiling salted water. Return to the boil, reduce heat and simmer for 15–20 minutes or until tender.

- Drain and leave to cool slightly before peeling and cutting into 0.5-cm (1/4-in) thick slices. Cover to keep warm.

- Trim French beans and slice into 4-cm (2-in) lengths. Boil in salted water for 8–10 minutes or until tender. Drain and cover to keep warm.

- Heat butter and sauté bacon strips and onion over high heat until lightly golden. Reduce heat and pour in wine vinegar. Simmer over low heat for 3 minutes, stirring occasionally. Season with salt and black pepper to taste.

- Combine French beans and sliced potatoes in a salad bowl. Pour bacon dressing over and toss gently until well mixed, taking care not to break up potato slices. Serve immediately.

curried
potato salad

A mildly spicy potato salad made up of potatoes, apples, celery and chopped bacon.

Serves 4

Ingredients

Potatoes	450 g (1 lb), scrubbed and unpeeled
Cider vinegar	1 tsp
Salt	to taste
Ground black pepper	to taste
Sour cream	150 ml (5 fl oz / $\frac{1}{2}$ cup)
Mayonnaise	70 ml (2$\frac{1}{3}$ fl oz / 5 Tbsp)
Curry powder	1–2 tsp
Lemon juice	2 tsp
Apples	2, peeled, cored and sliced
Celery	2 stalks, sliced
Bacon	2 rashers, cooked and chopped

Method

- Put potatoes into a pot of boiling salted water. Return to the boil, reduce heat and simmer for 15–20 minutes or until just tender. Drain and leave to cool. Peel and cut into 0.5-cm ($\frac{1}{4}$-in) thick slices.

- Toss potatoes gently with vinegar. Season with salt and pepper to taste.

- Combine sour cream, mayonnaise, curry powder and lemon juice. Mix well.

- Add apples, celery and bacon to potatoes. Pour sour cream and curry mixture over. Toss gently, taking care not to break up potatoes.

- Spoon salad into a serving dish. Chill for at least 1 hour before serving.

soups & appetisers

cream of potato soup

This filling soup makes a delicious appetiser served with hot slices of crusty bread.

Serves 4

Ingredients

Butter	50 g (1¾ oz)
Potatoes	450 g (1 lb), peeled and diced
Onions	2, large, peeled and finely chopped
Milk	435 ml (14 fl oz / 1¾ cups)
Vegetable or chicken stock	435 ml (14 fl oz / 1¾ cups)
Salt	to taste
Ground black pepper	to taste
Single cream	4 Tbsp
Finely chopped chives or parsley	
Croutons	

Method

- Heat butter and stir-fry potatoes and onions gently for about 5 minutes until onions are soft.
- Add milk and stock. Season with salt and pepper to taste and bring to the boil. Lower heat and simmer for 30 minutes, stirring occasionally, until potatoes are tender. Set aside to cool.
- Blend potato mixture in a food processor. Return soup to rinsed-out pan and reheat. Taste and adjust seasoning if necessary.
- Stir in cream just before serving. Garnish with chives or parsley, and croutons.

The flavour of this soup is vastly improved by using homemade stock, rather than a stock cube. Once cream has been added to soup, do not allow it to boil, otherwise cream will separate and spoil the appearance of the soup.

aloo ka shorva
(potato soup)

This is an Indian potato soup with a mild curry flavour.
Serves 6

Ingredients

Vegetable oil	2 Tbsp
Onion	1, peeled and finely chopped
Garlic	2 cloves, peeled and finely chopped
Potatoes	4, peeled and cut into small cubes plus $1/2$, peeled, grated and deep-fried
Curry powder	1 tsp
Salt	to taste
Water or vegetable stock	600 ml (19$1/3$ fl oz / 2$3/8$ cups)
Milk	250 ml (8 fl oz / 1cup)
Dried mint leaves	1 tsp

Method

- Heat oil in a pot. Stir-fry onion and garlic until softened.

- Add potato cubes, curry powder, salt and water or stock. Bring to the boil and reduce heat. Simmer for 20 minutes or until potatoes are cooked.

- Add milk and mint leaves. Simmer for another 5 minutes. Remove from the heat. Cool slightly, then purée in a blender.

- Reheat soup before serving. Sprinkle with fried grated potato and serve hot.

baby potatoes in dashi sauce

This is a tasty Japanese simmered dish with a flavourful sauce made with onions and dashi.

Serves 4

Ingredients

Sesame oil	1 Tbsp
Brown onion	1, small, peeled and thinly sliced
Baby potatoes	800 g (1¾ lb), unpeeled, washed, and scrubbed
Japanese soy sauce	2 Tbsp
Dashi	1 tsp dashi granules, mixed with 180 ml (6 fl oz / ¾ cup) water

Method

- Heat sesame oil and stir-fry onion for 1 minute. Add potatoes and mix well to ensure potatoes are well coated with sesame oil.

- Pour in soy sauce and dashi stock. Cover and simmer over low heat for 15 minutes. Turn potatoes over every now and then to ensure they are evenly cooked.

- Check that potatoes are cooked by piercing with a fork. Fork should go through easily.

- Transfer potatoes and onion to a serving bowl. Pour sauce over and serve immediately.

duchesse potatoes

These tasty potato rosettes complement roast meats and grilled steaks.

Serves 4

Ingredients

Potatoes	450 g (1 lb), peeled and thickly sliced
Butter	1 Tbsp
Egg	1, large, lightly beaten
Salt	to taste
Ground white pepper	to taste

Method

- Cover and cook potatoes in a pot of simmering salted water for 10 minutes, or until tender. Drain well and discard water in pot.

- To evaporate excess moisture in potatoes so that a more fluffy potato mixture can be obtained, return potatoes to dry pot and shake over low heat for 1–2 minutes. Shaking pot will prevent potatoes from sticking to the bottom of pot.

- Rub potatoes through a fine sieve, or press through a ricer. Add butter while potatoes are warm. Beat with a wooden spoon until mixture is very smooth. Mix egg gradually into potato mixture. Season with salt and pepper.

- Lightly oil a baking tray. Spoon potato mixture into a piping bag fitted with a 1-cm (¼-in) star nozzle and pipe rosettes onto baking tray.

- Bake in a preheated oven at 190°C (370°F) for 10–15 minutes, or until golden.

swiss potato rösti

This crisp yet creamy potato dish from Switzerland complements meat dishes and simple salads.

Serves 4–6

Ingredients

Potatoes	900 g (2 lb), scrubbed and unpeeled
Onion	1, peeled and finely chopped
Finely chopped parsley	2 Tbsp
Salt	to taste
Ground black pepper	to taste
Butter	55 g (2 oz)
Vegetable oil	
Finely chopped chives	1 tsp

Method

• Boil potatoes in lightly salted water for 15–20 minutes or until barely tender. Remove from heat and drain. Cool under cold running water and peel.

• Grate potatoes into a large bowl, using the coarsest blade of the grater. Mix in chopped onion, parsley, salt and pepper.

• Heat butter in a 23-cm (9-in) heavy-based frying pan. Add potato mixture and pat lightly into a large, flat and round cake with a spatula. Cook over low heat for 10–15 minutes or until the underside is crusty and browned.

• Grease a plate with oil. Using a spatula, turn rösti onto plate and slide it back onto the frying pan. Fry gently for another 10–15 minutes or until the underside is crisp and well-browned. Slide onto a warm serving dish. Garnish with a little chopped chives and serve immediately.

crêpes parmentier

These potato crêpes are named after Antoine-August Parmentier, who popularised the potato in France.

Serves 4

Ingredients

Plain (all-purpose) flour	55 g (2 oz)
Salt	
Egg	1, large, lightly beaten
Milk	75 ml (2½ fl oz / 5 Tbsp)
Butter	2 Tbsp, softened
Potatoes	225 g (8 oz), peeled
Ground black pepper	to taste
Olive oil	

Method

- Sift flour and a generous pinch of salt into a bowl. Make a well in the centre. Pour in lightly beaten egg and a little milk. Using a wooden spoon, beat mixture, gradually incorporating milk to make a smooth batter. Beat in remaining milk and 1 Tbsp butter. Cover and leave to stand for at least 30 minutes.

- Grate potatoes coarsely onto 2 or 3 layers of absorbent paper. Pat dry firmly with a tea towel to extract as much excess liquid as possible. Stir into prepared batter. Season generously with black pepper.

- Grease a large frying pan with olive oil. Add half the remaining butter, then spoon in 2 Tbsp potato batter for each crêpe, making 4 crêpes in pan. Keep crêpes well away from one another.

- Cook crêpes over gentle heat for about 5 minutes, or until undersides are golden. Turn over with a spatula and cook for another 5 minutes, or until crisp and golden.

- Transfer crêpes to a heated serving plate and keep warm. Add remaining butter to pan and cook remaining batter as above. Serve immediately.

roasted potato chips

These garlic-flavoured roasted chips are delicious with grilled meats or omelettes.

Serves 4–6

Ingredients

Olive oil	2 Tbsp
Garlic	3 cloves, crushed
Potatoes	900 g (2 lb)
Fresh thyme	3 stalks, leaves stripped off for use and stems discarded
Salt	to taste
Ground black pepper	to taste

Method

- Combine oil and garlic in a large and shallow roasting tin. Place in preheated oven at 220°C (425°F) for 5 minutes.

- Scrub potatoes and cut into 1 x 3-cm ($^1/_2$ x 1$^1/_2$-in) lengths. Pat dry with paper towels.

- Remove roasting tin from oven and put over low heat on top of hob. Add potatoes and toss with thyme in hot oil until well coated. Return to oven and roast for 40 minutes until golden brown.

- Season with salt and black pepper to taste before serving.

Leaving the potatoes unpeeled adds extra flavour to the dish.

crunchy potato skins

This is a popular American dish commonly served before a course of thick juicy burgers and salad.

Serves 4

Ingredients

Potatoes	4, large, scrubbed
Sour cream	225 ml (7$\frac{1}{3}$ fl oz / $\frac{7}{8}$ cup)
Finely chopped chives	2 Tbsp
Salt	to taste
Ground black pepper	to taste
Vegetable oil	
Mayonnaise	4 Tbsp

Method

- Prick potatoes all over with a fork. Bake at 200°C (400°F) for 1 hour to 1 hour 30 minutes, or until tender. Remove and leave to cool slightly. Cut each potato in half, lengthways. Scoop out the flesh, leaving a layer of 0.5-cm ($\frac{1}{4}$-in) thick flesh on skin *(see note)*. Slice potato skins in half, lengthways again.

- To make dip, mix sour cream and 1 Tbsp chives together. Add salt and pepper to taste. Spoon into a serving bowl and refrigerate.

- Heat oil to 190°C (375°F) and deep-fry potato skins for 2–3 minutes until brown and crisp. Drain and arrange on a serving plate.

- Sprinkle with plenty of salt and garnish each potato skin with 1 tsp mayonnaise and remaining chives. Serve immediately with sour cream dip.

NOTE

Leftover cooked potato flesh may be mashed with plenty of butter and used as a topping for pies.

lemon
potatoes

A baked Mediterranean potato dish with the tangy flavour of lemon.
Serves 4

Ingredients

Potatoes	900 g (2 lb), medium, peeled and cut into thick slices
Lemon	1, grated for zest and squeezed for juice
Salt	to taste
Ground black pepper	to taste
Butter	55 g (2 oz)
Lemon slices	

Method

• Place potato slices in a gratin dish. Sprinkle with grated lemon zest and half the juice. Season generously with salt and black pepper. Dot butter over the surface and bake in a preheated oven at 190°C (375°F) for 15 minutes.

• Drain excess fat from dish and sprinkle with remaining lemon juice. Toss potatoes and bake for another 20–25 minutes or until slightly brown and tender.

• Transfer to a heated serving dish using a slotted spoon. Garnish with lemon slices and a little grated lemon zest. Serve immediately.

potato gratin

This creamy potato gratin with cheese is one of the classic dishes in French cuisine.

Serves 4

Ingredients

Potatoes	4, large, washed and peeled
Eggs	3, well beaten
Double cream	425 ml (14 fl oz / 1¾ cups)
Gruyère cheese	55 g (2 oz), grated
Parmesan cheese	55 g (2 oz), grated
Salt	to taste
Ground black pepper	to taste
Grated nutmeg	a pinch

Topping

Gruyère cheese	55 g (2 oz), grated
Butter	30 g (1 oz), diced

Method

- Slice potatoes to 0.5-cm (¼-in) thickness.
- Beat eggs with double cream in a large mixing bowl. Beat in grated Gruyère and Parmesan cheese. Season with salt, pepper and nutmeg to taste. Add sliced potatoes to mixture. Mix well to ensure potato slices are evenly coated.
- Pour potato mixture into a buttered 20 x 28-cm (8 x 11-in) gratin dish. Top with grated Gruyère cheese and dot with diced butter.
- Bake in a preheated oven at 150°C (300°F) for 1 hour 20 minutes to 1 hour 30 minutes, or until potatoes are tender. Serve immediately.

potato puri
(fried potato bread)

This Indian potato bread is light and puffy when cooked. Serve immediately after frying.

Serves 8

Ingredients

Potatoes	250 g (9 oz)
Plain (all-purpose) flour	240 g (8½ oz)
Salt	2 tsp
Warm water	90–105 ml (3–3½ fl oz / 6–7 Tbsp)
Cooking oil for deep-frying	

Method

• Peel potatoes and boil until tender. Drain and return to a dry saucepan over very low heat for a few minutes to dry out thoroughly. Mash well and leave to cool.

• Sift flour and salt into a bowl. Add mashed potatoes. Mix with a wooden spoon and add water, a little at a time, until a firm dough is formed. Knead thoroughly on a board or table top with well-floured hands for 5–10 minutes.

• Roll dough into a ball. Cover and leave to stand for at least 30 minutes *(see note)*. Divide into 16 even pieces. Roll each piece into a small ball and flatten. Roll out into 15-cm (7½-in) rounds.

• Heat oil until very hot. Slide a puri in and immediately start spooning oil over the topside so that it puffs up. As soon as puri is golden on the underside, flip over and cook until the other side is golden.

• Drain and serve hot with curries, dhal or vegetables.

NOTE

Dough can be prepared in advance, wrapped in cling film (plastic wrap) and kept refrigerated for several hours.

spicy potato and pea bhaji

An Indian vegetarian dish of potatoes and peas cooked with green chilli and curry spices.

Serves 4

Ingredients

Vegetable oil	3–4 Tbsp
Onion	1, peeled and thinly sliced
Ground turmeric	1 tsp
Ground cumin	1 tsp
Finely grated ginger	¼ tsp
Green chilli	1, halved, seeded and finely chopped
Potatoes	450 g (1 lb), peeled and diced
Frozen peas	250 g (9 oz), blanched in hot water for 2 minutes

Method

- Heat oil and stir-fry onion over medium heat for 5–7 minutes until brown but not crisp. Reduce heat and stir in turmeric, cumin, ginger, chilli and potatoes. Stir-fry for another 5 minutes.

- Transfer onion and potato mixture to a casserole dish. Add peas and mix well.

- Cover and bake in a preheated oven at 180°C (350°F) for 15–20 minutes or until potatoes are tender. Transfer to a small serving bowl and serve hot.

dry potato takari

This fragrant Indian potato dish is cooked with tomatoes and curry spices.

Serves 6

Ingredients

Cooking oil	125 ml (4 fl oz / ½ cup)
Mustard seeds	1 tsp
Potatoes	4, large, peeled and diced
Onion	1, peeled and chopped
Salt	2 tsp
Ground turmeric	2 tsp
Water	125 ml (4 fl oz / ½ cup)
Chilli powder	2 tsp
Sugar	1 tsp
Chopped coriander leaves (cilantro)	1 tsp
Lemon juice	1 Tbsp
Tomatoes	3, medium, sliced
Garam masala	1 tsp

Method

- Heat oil and stir-fry mustard seeds over medium heat. Be careful and use a lid if necessary as mustard seeds will pop. When mustard seeds begin to pop, add diced potatoes, onion, salt and turmeric powder. Fry until potatoes turn light brown.

- Add 90 ml (3 fl oz / ⅜ cup) water, chilli powder and sugar. Fry until mixture becomes dry. Add remaining water. Cover and simmer until potatoes are tender.

- Add coriander leaves and lemon juice. Cook until mixture turns dry. Add tomato slices. Stir in garam masala and mix well. Remove from heat and serve.

crunchy curried potatoes

Serve these spicy potatoes with a meat dish.

Serves 4

Ingredients

Potatoes	700 g (1½ lb), cut into large chunks
Vegetable oil	2 Tbsp
Margarine or butter	30 g (1 oz)
Mild curry powder	1 Tbsp, mixed with 1 Tbsp water
Salt	to taste
Ground black pepper	to taste
Lemon	½, juice extracted

Method

- Place potatoes in a pot of salted water. Bring to the boil, then reduce heat and simmer for about 15 minutes until potatoes are almost tender. Drain and arrange in a single layer in a lightly greased ovenproof dish.
- Heat oil and margarine. Add curry powder mixture and stir-fry for 1 minute over medium heat. Coat potatoes evenly with curry powder mixture. Season with salt and pepper.
- Bake in a preheated oven at 200°C (400°F) for 25 minutes, then turn potatoes over and bake for another 15 minutes, until tender and crisp. Sprinkle with lemon juice and serve immediately.

snacks

potato wedges with tarragon dip

This is a tasty snack of crisp chunks of baked potatoes served with a refreshing dip.

Serves 4

Ingredients

Potatoes	4, medium
Cooking oil	45 ml (1 fl oz / 3 Tbsp)
Barbecue seasoning	1 Tbsp

Dip

Fromage frais	150 ml (5 fl oz / $^5/_8$ cup)
Lemon juice	$^1/_2$, juice extracted
Dried tarragon	3 Tbsp

Method

- Scrub potatoes and cut into 6–8 wedges lengthways. Combine oil and barbecue seasoning in a mixing bowl. Dip potato wedges in mixture and drain slightly on absorbent paper.

- Arrange wedges on a wire rack on a baking tray. Bake in a preheated oven at 200°C (400°F) for about 20 minutes or until well browned and crisp.

- To make dip, combine all ingredients in a food processor for 30 seconds, or beat together in a bowl. Transfer to a small serving bowl and serve with potato wedges.

If you want to spice up the tarragon dip a little, add some cayenne pepper, or a crushed clove of garlic. Pieces of well-grilled bacon may also be added to the dip as a variation.

cheese and potato scones

These delicious savoury scones are perfect for afternoon tea.

Serves 8–10

Ingredients

Self-raising flour	100 g (3$\frac{1}{2}$ oz), grated
Baking powder	2 tsp
Salt	$\frac{1}{4}$ tsp
Mustard powder	a pinch
Butter	30 g (1 oz), diced
Mature Cheddar cheese	100 g (3$\frac{1}{2}$ oz), grated
Potatoes	100 g (3$\frac{1}{2}$ oz), boiled, peeled, mashed and cooled
Egg	1, small
Milk	1 Tbsp
Vegetable oil	

Method

- Sift flour, baking powder, salt and mustard powder into a mixing bowl. Rub in butter until mixture resembles breadcrumbs. Stir in cheese until thoroughly mixed.

- Sieve mashed potatoes into flour mixture and mix together with a round-bladed knife. Beat egg with milk, and pour slowly into potato mixture while mixing, adding just enough liquid to form a soft dough.

- Turn dough out onto a well-floured surface and knead lightly. Roll dough into a 2-cm (1-in) thick sheet and using a 5-cm (2$\frac{1}{2}$-in) round cutter, cut out scones.

- Place scones on a greased baking tray. Bake in a preheated oven at 190°C (375°F) for 15 minutes until golden brown. Cool for a few minutes on a wire rack, then serve warm.

potato ramekins

A baked mashed potato dish with a crunchy topping of breadcrumbs.

Serves 4

Ingredients

Potatoes	450 g (1 lb), peeled
Milk	1 Tbsp
Butter	70 g (2$\frac{1}{2}$ oz)
Salt	to taste
Ground black pepper	to taste
Chopped parsley	1 tsp
Chopped basil	$\frac{1}{2}$ tsp
Parmesan cheese	55 g (2 oz), grated
Fresh white breadcrumbs	25 g (1 oz)

Method

- Place potatoes in a pot of boiling salted water. Return to the boil, lower heat and simmer for 15–20 minutes or until tender. Drain well.
- Add milk and 55 g (2 oz) butter to potatoes and mash. Mix until smooth, then season with salt and black pepper to taste.
- Stir parsley, basil and cheese into potato mixture. Spoon into ramekin dishes. Do not allow potato mixture to get cold.
- Top ramekins with breadcrumbs and dot with remaining butter. Place under a preheated grill for 3 minutes until tops are golden. Serve immediately.

Ready-grated packets of Parmesan cheese are easily available from supermarkets. Alternatively, use a strong Cheddar.

tortilla with chorizo sausage

This substantial egg and potato dish of Spanish origin may be served together with a salad of sliced peppers and crusty bread.

Serves 4

Ingredients

Olive oil	60 ml (2 fl oz / ¼ cup)
Onions	2, peeled and sliced
Potatoes	450 g (1 lb), peeled and cut into 1-cm (½-in) cubes
Chorizo sausages	170 g (6 oz), cut into 1-cm (½-in) cubes
Eggs	6
Salt	to taste
Ground black pepper	to taste
Finely chopped parsley	2 Tbsp

Method

- Heat oil in a heavy-based frying pan over medium heat. Stir-fry onions for 3 minutes. Reduce to low heat and add potatoes. Cover and cook for 15–20 minutes, or until potatoes are soft, stirring occasionally.

- Stir in chorizo sausages and cook for 2–3 minutes. Beat eggs together with salt, pepper and 1½ Tbsp parsley.

- Pour eggs over potato and sausage mixture in frying pan. Cover and leave to cook over a low heat for about 20 minutes, or until eggs are set.

- Invert tortilla onto a warmed serving plate. Cut into wedges to serve, garnished with remaining parsley.

NOTE

Chorizo is a spicy Spanish sausage made from minced pork spiced with paprika. There are two types, one that requires cooking and one that is ready to eat. Use the ready-to-eat sausage for this dish, or use salami as a substitute.

potato and carrot layer

A flavourful dish of mashed potatoes, carrots, sultanas and walnuts.
Serves 6

Ingredients

Potatoes	1.4 kg (3 lb 1 oz)
Milk	3 Tbsp
Butter	30 g (1 oz)
Salt	to taste
Ground black pepper	to taste
Onion	1, peeled and chopped
Carrots	700 g (1 1/2 lb), peeled and cut into 1-cm (1/2-in) cubes
Walnuts	55 g (2 oz), shelled and chopped
Lemon juice	1 Tbsp
Water	1 Tbsp
Sultanas	55 g (2 oz)

Method

- Cook potatoes in boiling salted water for about 15 minutes or until tender. Drain and peel. Add milk and half the butter. Mash well. Season with salt and pepper to taste.

- Heat remaining butter and fry onion gently until soft. Stir in carrots, walnuts, lemon juice, water and sultanas. Simmer gently for 10 minutes until carrots are just tender. Season with salt and pepper to taste and remove from heat.

- Grease a large ovenproof dish. Spread half the mashed potatoes in dish and top with carrot mixture. Top with remaining mashed potatoes. Bake in a preheated oven at 190°C (375°F) for 15–20 minutes. Garnish with sultanas and walnuts. Serve immediately.

ham and potato cakes

These are patties of pan-fried grated potatoes with a crunchy topping of breadcrumbs and savoury ham.

Serves 4

Ingredients

Potatoes	450 g (1 lb), peeled, grated
Onion	1, large, finely chopped
Cooked ham	100 g (3$\frac{1}{2}$ oz), sliced and chopped
Salt	to taste
Ground black pepper	to taste
Butter	75 g (2$\frac{1}{2}$ oz)
Fresh white breadcrumbs	55 g (2 oz)
Finely chopped parsley	1 Tbsp
Cheddar cheese	30 g (1 oz), grated

Method

- Combine grated potatoes and onion. Place in a colander or a large sieve and squeeze out all excess liquid.

- Put potato and onion mixture into a mixing bowl. Mix in half the chopped ham and season well with salt and pepper. Divide into 4 portions and shape into 10-cm (5-in) rounds.

- Heat 45 g (1$\frac{1}{2}$ oz) butter in a large frying pan. Cook ham and potato cakes over medium heat for 8–10 minutes on each side, or until golden and cooked through.

- Heat remaining butter in another saucepan. Stir-fry breadcrumbs for about 10 minutes over low heat until crisp and golden. Remove from heat.

- Add remaining chopped ham, parsley and grated cheese to fried breadcrumbs. Spoon mixture equally over the top of each potato cake. Serve immediately.

potato and spinach croquettes

For a tasty alternative to chips, try these crispy croquettes with a creamy potato and spinach filling.

Serves 4–6

Ingredients

Potatoes	450 g (1 lb), peeled and cut into large, even-sized pieces
Spinach	450 g (1 lb)
Egg yolk	1, lightly beaten
Grated mature Cheddar cheese	2 Tbsp
Salt	to taste
Ground black pepper	to taste
Plain (all-purpose) flour	3 Tbsp, seasoned with salt and ground black pepper to taste
Eggs	2, lightly beaten
Dry white breadcrumbs	75 g (2½ oz)
Vegetable oil	for deep-frying

Method

- Place potatoes in a pot of salted water. Bring to the boil, then reduce heat and simmer for 15 minutes, or until potatoes are tender. Drain well and rub through a sieve to purée.

- Rinse spinach and place it, still wet, in a large saucepan. Cover and cook over low heat for 5 minutes or until tender, stirring occasionally. Drain well and chop finely.

- Place potato purée and spinach in a large bowl. Beat in egg yolk and cheese. Season with salt and black pepper to taste. On a floured surface, roll potato mixture into fat sausage shapes, about 5 cm (2½-in) long.

- Coat each croquette evenly in flour, followed by beaten eggs and breadcrumbs.

- Heat oil to 180°C (350°F) and deep-fry croquettes in batches, for 2 minutes, or until golden brown. Drain well and serve hot.

new potatoes and fennel

This dish of baked new potatoes is infused with the aromatic flavour of chopped fennel.

Serves 4–6

Ingredients

Butter	70 g (2$\frac{1}{2}$ oz)
Sweet paprika	$\frac{1}{2}$ tsp
Baby potatoes	900 g (2 lb), washed, dried and unpeeled
Fennel bulb	1, small, finely chopped
Mint leaves	2 sprigs, finely chopped
Fennel leaves	

Method

- Heat butter in a baking dish over low heat. Stir in paprika and add potatoes. Sauté for about 4 minutes until potatoes begin to brown on all sides.

- Cover baking dish with a lid or aluminium foil. Bake in a preheated oven at 180°C (350°F) for 25 minutes. Remove from oven, then add chopped fennel and mint leaves. Mix together gently. Replace cover and return to oven. Continue to cook for another 15 minutes.

- Remove baking dish from oven and stir potatoes, being careful not to cut potato skins. Garnish with fennel leaves and serve immediately.

indonesian potato cutlets

These are fragrant potato patties made from a mixture of mashed potatoes and shallots. They are great as a teatime snack.

Makes 8–10

Ingredients

Potatoes	500 g (1 lb 1½ oz), unpeeled
Shallots	6, peeled and finely sliced
Salt	½ tsp
Ground white pepper	to taste
Spring onion (scallion)	1, finely sliced
Egg	1, beaten
Cooking oil for deep-frying	

Method

- Place potatoes in a pot of water and bring to the boil. Reduce heat and simmer for 20 minutes or until potatoes are cooked and tender. Cool slightly, then peel and mash roughly.

- Heat oil and fry shallots until golden brown. Drain well and add to mashed potatoes together with salt, pepper and spring onion. Mix well. Leave to cool before forming into 8 balls.

- Flatten balls into cutlets, each about 2 cm (1-in) thick. Heat oil to 180°C (350°F). Dip potato cutlets into beaten egg and deep-fry for about 2–3 minutes, or until golden brown. Drain well and serve.

potato gnocchi with broccoli

Tiny potato dumplings served as an alternative to pasta in some parts of Italy.

Serves 4–6

Ingredients

Potatoes	700 g (1½ lb), peeled and cut into chunks
Egg	1, beaten
Plain (all-purpose) flour	55 g (2 oz), sifted
Parmesan cheese	55 g (2 oz), freshly grated
Ground black pepper	to taste
Salt	to taste
Ground nutmeg	to taste
Broccoli florets	225 g (8 oz), steamed until tender
Butter	55 g (2 oz)
Single cream	150 ml (5 fl oz / ⅝ cup)

Method

- Steam potatoes for 20 minutes or until tender. When cooked, rub through a sieve into a large mixing bowl. Add egg, flour and 25 g (1 oz) parmesan cheese to potatoes. Blend well. Add salt, black pepper and nutmeg to taste.

- Roll some potato mixture on a well-floured surface into a long roll 2-cm (1-in) in diameter. Cut into 2-cm (1-in) lengths and flatten slightly, using the back of a fork. Repeat until potato mixture is used up.

- Place broccoli florets in an ovenproof dish and dot with butter. Keep warm in a 150°C (300°F) oven.

- Bring a large pot of water to a gentle simmer. Drop gnocchi in, about 10 at a time. When gnocchi floats to the surface after a few seconds, remove with slotted spoon and place in ovenproof dish with broccoli florets. Keep warm while cooking remainder.

- Drizzle gnocchi and broccoli with cream and mix very gently. Sprinkle with remaining cheese and place dish under a hot grill for 5 minutes or until cheese is beginning to brown. Serve immediately, lightly sprinkled with black pepper.

crispy tuna jackets

The potato jackets are made extra crispy by rubbing them with olive oil.

Serves 4

Ingredients

Potatoes	4, large, scrubbed and pat dry
Olive oil	
Butter	30 g (1 oz)
Canned tuna	200 g (7 oz), in brine, drained
Celery	2 stalks, halved lengthways and finely chopped
Chopped chives	4 Tbsp
Cheddar cheese	175 g (6 oz), finely grated
Salt	to taste
Ground black pepper	to taste

Method

- Prick potatoes all over with a fork, and rub olive oil all over skins. Bake in a preheated oven at 190°C (375°F) for 1 hour to 1 hour 15 minutes, or until skins are very crisp and flesh is tender.

- Remove potatoes from oven. When cool enough to handle, cut a slice off the top of each potato lengthways. Scoop out flesh into a mixing bowl, taking care not to pierce skins. Set skins aside.

- Add butter to potato flesh and mash lightly with a fork. Stir in tuna, celery, chives and 100 g (3 1/2 oz) cheese. Season with salt and pepper to taste. Mix well.

- Divide potato filling roughly into 4 portions. Spoon a portion into each potato skin, pressing it down so that skins are well filled. Pile into a mound on top. Sprinkle with remaining cheese.

- Cook in preheated grill for about 2 minutes or until cheese turns golden brown. Serve immediately.

samosas

These are crispy triangular Indian pastries filled with spiced potatoes and peas.

Makes 15–18

Ingredients

Potatoes	450 g (1 lb), unpeeled
Cooking oil for deep-frying	
Onion	$\frac{1}{2}$, peeled and minced
Frozen peas	110 g (4 oz), blanched in hot water for 2 minutes
Finely grated ginger	2 tsp
Green chilli	$\frac{1}{2}$, finely chopped
Finely chopped coriander leaves (cilantro)	2 Tbsp
Water	45 ml (1$\frac{1}{2}$ fl oz / 3 Tbsp)
Curry powder	3 Tbsp
Salt	1 tsp
Lemon juice	1$\frac{1}{2}$ Tbsp
Spring roll skin	5–6 sheets, 21.5 x 21.5-cm (11 x 11-in)
Corn flour (cornstarch) mixture	1 Tbsp, mixed with 2 Tbsp water

Method

- Cover potatoes with water in a pot and bring to the boil. Reduce heat and simmer for 20 minutes or until potatoes are cooked and tender. Drain well. When cool, peel and cut into 1-cm ($\frac{1}{2}$-in) cubes.

- Heat 2$\frac{1}{2}$ Tbsp oil and stir-fry onion until translucent. Add peas, ginger, green chilli, chopped coriander leaves and water. Stir-fry for another 2 minutes.

- Add potato cubes, curry powder, salt and lemon juice. Mix well gently and stir-fry over low heat for 3–4 minutes. Set aside to cool.

- Cut each square sheet of spring roll skin into 3 equal strips. To make samosa, position one rectangular strip of spring roll skin with breadth facing you. Place 1 Tbsp potato mixture on the lower portion of strip, leaving a 2.5-cm (1-in) margin from the edge. Fold the lower left hand corner of strip diagonally across to form an isosceles triangle. Fold over in a zig-zag pattern, maintaining the form of an isosceles triangle until the top of the sheet is reached, where a small corner of spring roll skin remains. Dab with corn flour mixture and fold over to seal.

- Heat oil to 180°C (350°F) and deep-fry samosas until golden brown and crisp. Drain well and serve.

chicken curry puffs

Curried potato and chicken cubes encased in golden brown puff pastry. Makes 20–24

Ingredients

Ready rolled frozen puff pastry	5–6 sheets, cut into quarters
Egg	1, lightly beaten

Filling

Cooking oil for frying	
Onions	330 g (12 oz), peeled and diced
Potatoes	330 g (12 oz), peeled and diced
Salt	1/4 tsp
Chicken stock	180 ml (6 fl oz / 3/4 cup)
Chopped ginger	1 tsp
Garlic	2 cloves, peeled and chopped
Shallots	8, peeled and minced
Chicken	450 g (1 lb), cut into small cubes
Curry powder	4 heaped Tbsp

Seasoning

Sugar	1/2 Tbsp
Salt	2 tsp

Method

- Heat 1 Tbsp oil and fry onions until translucent. Set aside. Heat another 1 Tbsp oil and stir-fry potatoes with salt over high heat for 5 minutes. Stir in 125 ml (4 fl oz / 1/2 cup) chicken stock. Cover and cook over moderate heat until potatoes are cooked. Remove and set aside.

- Heat 2 Tbsp oil in a clean wok and stir-fry ginger, garlic and shallots until brown. Add chicken cubes and stir-fry for 5 minutes. Add curry powder and stir-fry for another 5 minutes. Return fried onions and potatoes to frying pan and mix well. Add remaining chicken stock and seasoning. Reduce heat and cook until almost dry, stirring occasionally. Set aside to cool.

- Place 1 Tbsp filling in the centre of each small square of pastry. Moisten edges with water and fold over diagonally to seal and form a triangular puff. Press along edges with the back of a fork to form a pattern.

- Arrange curry puffs on a greased baking tray. Glaze with egg and bake in a preheated oven at 220°C (440°F) for 5 minutes. Reduce to 200°C (400°F) and bake for another 15–20 minutes or until golden brown. Cool on a wire rack before serving.

japanese potato croquettes

This is a crispy snack dish with a hearty filling of mashed potatoes, minced beef and onions.

Serves 4–8

Ingredients

Potatoes	450 g (1 lb), unpeeled
Cooking oil for deep-frying	
Brown onion	1/2, peeled and minced
Minced beef	100 g (3 1/2 oz)
Salt	to taste
Ground black pepper	to taste
Eggs	2, lightly beaten in separate bowls
Plain (all-purpose) flour	70 g (2 1/2 oz)
Dried breadcrumbs	140 g (5 oz)
Lemon	1, cut into 8 wedges
Cabbage	4 leaves, finely shredded

Method

- Cover potatoes with water in a large pot and bring to the boil. Reduce heat and simmer for 20 minutes or until potatoes are cooked and tender. Drain well. When cool, peel and mash.

- Heat 2 Tbsp oil and sauté minced onion with beef. Season to taste with salt and pepper. Remove from heat and set aside. When cool, mix well with mashed potatoes and a beaten egg.

- Divide potato mixture into 8 equal portions. Shape into patties about 1-cm (1/2-in) thick. Coat each croquette with flour, followed by remaining beaten egg and breadcrumbs.

- Heat oil to 180°C (350°F) and deep-fry croquettes until golden brown. Drain well. Serve with lemon wedges and shredded cabbage.

potato-stuffed pancakes

A substantial Indian pancake with a spiced potato filling. Suitable for vegetarians.

Serves 6

Ingredients

Filling

Cooking oil	2 Tbsp
Mustard seeds	$\frac{1}{2}$ tsp
Onion	1, peeled and finely sliced
Green chilli	1, finely sliced
Ginger	2.5-cm (1-in) knob, finely sliced
Ground turmeric	$\frac{1}{2}$ tsp
Curry leaves	a few
Potatoes	4, peeled, boiled and mashed
Onions	2, boiled for 10 minutes, peeled and finely sliced.
Salt	to taste

Pancakes

Split black beans	100 g ($3\frac{1}{2}$ oz), washed and soaked in cold water overnight
Rice flour	250 g (9 oz)
Baking powder	1 tsp
Salt	to taste
Water	300–450 ml (10–14 fl oz / $1\frac{1}{4}$–$1\frac{3}{4}$ cups)
Cooking oil for frying	250 ml (8 fl oz/ 1 cup)

Method

- To prepare pancakes, drain beans and grind to a paste with rice flour in a food processor. Place mixture in a large bowl. Cover and leave in a cool place for at least 8 hours. Just before use, add baking powder and salt, with sufficient water to make a thick batter the consistency of heavy cream.

- Heat 1 Tbsp oil in a heavy-based frying pan and spoon 1 Tbsp batter into the centre. Spread batter gently in a circular motion to form a 12-cm (6- in) round. Cook for 2–3 minutes, on one side only. Remove carefully and place onto a clean tea towel. Repeat to make more pancakes until all the batter is used up. Add more oil to pan as necessary.

- To prepare filling, heat oil and sauté mustard seeds until they 'pop'. Add raw onion slices, green chilli, ginger, turmeric and curry leaves. Stir-fry mixture until onion slices turn brown.

- Add mashed potatoes and boiled onion slices. Mix well and add salt to taste. Stir-fry for another 1–2 minutes. Remove from heat.

- Place 1 Tbsp potato mixture onto the centre of each pancake and fold over filling. Serve immediately, or pan-fry filled pancakes quickly on both sides to crisp them before serving.

main dishes

fidgett pie

Topped with shortcrust pastry, this pie is filled wth potato and apple slices, onions and pieces of bacon.

Serves 4

Ingredients

Frozen shortcrust pastry	175 g (6 oz), defrosted
Potatoes	225 g (8 oz), peeled and sliced thinly
Dessert apples	225 g (8 oz), peeled and sliced
Onions	225 g (8 oz), peeled and chopped
Uncooked gammon or bacon rashers	350 g (12$\frac{1}{2}$ oz), diced into 1-cm ($\frac{1}{2}$-in) pieces
Salt	to taste
Ground black pepper	to taste
Ground nutmeg	to taste
Chicken stock	150 ml (4$\frac{1}{2}$ fl oz / $\frac{1}{2}$ cup), chilled
Egg	1, beaten

Method

- Roll out pastry to fit the top of an 850 ml (27$\frac{1}{2}$ fl oz / 3$\frac{3}{8}$ cups) pie dish. Reserve excess pastry to decorate pie.

- Line the bottom of dish with potatoes. Layer apples, onions and gammon or bacon on top. Season to taste with salt, pepper and nutmeg. If apples are slightly tart, sprinkle with a little sugar before use. Pour in stock.

- Cover with pastry and decorate with shapes cut out from trimmings. Poke a small hole in the top crust to allow steam to escape when pie is baking. Glaze with beaten egg.

- Bake in a preheated oven at 200°C (400°F) for 15 minutes. Cover with foil to prevent the pastry from getting too brown and bake at 180°C (350°F) for another 45 minutes. Serve immediately.

chunky vegetable pie

A crusty pie filled with potato cubes and assorted vegetables.

Serves 6

Ingredients

Butter	30 g (1 oz)
Onion	1, peeled and chopped
Plain (all-purpose) flour	30 g (1 oz)
Milk	300 ml (10 fl oz / 1 1/4 cups)
Mustard seeds	2 Tbsp
Ground black pepper	to taste
Salt	to taste
Potatoes	2, large, peeled and cubed
Carrot	1, peeled and cubed
Cauliflower florets	175 g (6 oz)
Frozen peas	100 g (3 1/2 oz), defrosted
Corn kernels	100 g (3 1/2 oz) or 225 g (8 oz) swede, peeled and cubed
Frozen shortcrust pastry	225 g (8 oz), defrosted
Egg	1, beaten
White sesame seeds	1 Tbsp

Method

- To make sauce, heat butter and fry onion until soft. Add flour and stir-fry for 3 minutes. Increase heat and gradually add milk. Stir until mixture boils and thickens. Reduce heat and simmer for another 3–4 minutes. Stir in mustard seeds and season with pepper and salt to taste. Set aside to cool.

- Cook potatoes and carrot in boiling water for 5 minutes. Add cauliflower florets and boil until vegetables are barely tender. Add peas and corn kernels or swede. Cook for another 1 minute. Drain all vegetables and stir into sauce. Spoon mixture into a 1.1 litre (35 1/3 fl oz / 4 1/2 cup) ovenproof dish.

- Roll out shortcrust pastry to 0.5-cm (1/4-in) thickness on a floured surface and cut a piece to layer over and cover pie. Trim off any excess pastry. Glaze with beaten egg and sprinkle with sesame seeds.

- Press around the rim of pie dish and poke a small hole in the centre of top crust to allow steam to escape when pie is baking. Bake in a preheated oven at 180°C (350°F) for 40 minutes or until golden brown. Serve hot.

golden fish pie

A homey baked dish of fish fillets topped with creamy mashed potatoes.

Serves 4

Ingredients

Firm white fish fillets (e.g. cod or haddock)	450 g (1 lb), skinned and deboned
Smoked fish fillets (e.g. cod or haddock)	450 g (1 lb), skinned and deboned
Milk	475 ml (15¼ fl oz / 1¾ cups)
Fennel seeds	2 tsp
Black peppercorns	6
Bay leaves	2
Onion	¼, peeled and roughly sliced
Butter	100 g (3½ oz)
Plain (all-purpose) flour	45 g (1½ oz)
Chopped fresh parsley	2 Tbsp
Salt	to taste
Ground black pepper	to taste
Potatoes	700 g (1½ lb), peeled and cut into even-sized pieces

Method

• Place fresh and smoked fish in a shallow ovenproof dish. Add milk, fennel seeds, peppercorns, bay leaves and onion slices. Cover and bake in a preheated oven at 180°C (350°F) for 25–30 minutes. Remove fish and flake into smaller pieces in a bowl. Strain milky liquid and discard fennel seeds, bay leaves, peppercorns and onions.

• Melt 45 g (1½ oz) butter in a saucepan over low heat. Add flour and gradually stir in strained milky liquid. Bring to the boil and stir until sauce thickens. Stir in chopped parsley and pour over fish. Mix well and season with salt and pepper to taste. Spoon mixture into a 1.4 litre (45 fl oz / 5½ cup) ovenproof dish. Set aside.

• Cover potatoes with water in a large pot and bring to the boil. Simmer until cooked and tender. Drain well. Add remaining butter and milk. Mash until smooth.

• Spoon mashed potatoes over fish mixture. Smoothen surface with the back of a spoon, then run a fork across the surface to leave a wavy pattern on top.

• Increase oven temperature to 200°C (400°F) and bake for 30–40 minutes, or until golden.

ham charlotte

A baked dish with alternating layers of potato slices, ham and mushrooms in cheese sauce.

Serves 4

Ingredients

Butter	15 g (½ oz)
Button mushrooms	70 g (2½ oz), wiped and sliced
Cooked ham	100 g (3½ oz), minced in processor
Cooked potatoes	225 g (8 oz), sliced
Fresh white breadcrumbs	100 g (3½ oz)
Cheddar cheese	70 g (2½ oz), grated

Cheese sauce

Butter	30 g (1 oz)
Plain (all-purpose) flour	30 g (1 oz)
Milk	300 ml (10 fl oz / 1¼ cups)
Cheddar cheese	45–55 g (1½–2 oz), grated
Mustard powder	½ tsp
Salt	to taste
Ground black pepper	to taste

Method

- To make cheese sauce, melt butter over low heat in a saucepan. Remove from heat and stir in flour. Return to low heat and stir gently for 1–2 minutes until smooth. Continue to stir and add milk a little at a time. When well-blended, bring sauce to the boil while stirring continuously. Reduce to low heat and add cheese, mustard powder, salt and pepper. Cover and simmer for 5 minutes. Set aside.

- Melt butter and sauté mushrooms lightly. Mix with ham and stir in cheese sauce. Place a layer of ham and cheese mixture in the base of an ovenproof dish. Cover with sliced potatoes. Repeat layering with ham and cheese mixture and potatoes, ending with potatoes as the final layer.

- Mix breadcrumbs and grated cheese together. Sprinkle over the top. Bake in the centre of a preheated oven at 200°C (400°F) for 20 minutes, or until top is golden and cheese is bubbling.

tiddy oggies

These are delicious potato pasties with a rich shortcrust pastry.

Makes 10

Ingredients

Pastry

Plain (all-purpose) flour	400 g (14 oz)
Salt	1 tsp
Butter	200 g (7 oz)
Water	150 ml (5 fl oz / ⁵⁄₈ cup)
Egg yolk	1, beaten

Filling

Braising beef steak	400 g (14 oz), finely diced
Strong beef stock	150 ml (5 fl oz / ⁵⁄₈ cup)
Potatoes	500 g (1 lb 1 oz), peeled and finely diced
Onions	250 g (9 oz), peeled and chopped
Corn kernels	100 g (3½ oz) or 225 g (8 oz) swede, peeled and cubed
Salt	2 tsp
Ground black pepper	1 tsp

Method

- To make pastry, sift flour and salt into a mixing bowl. Rub in butter until mixture resembles breadcrumbs. Add a little water at a time and knead to achieve a firm dough. Knead until smooth.

- Mix all ingredients for filling together in a large bowl.

- Divide pastry into 10 equal portions. Roll out each piece and cut into an 11.5-cm (5¼-in) round, using a plate or pan lid as a guide.

- Divide filling equally among pastry rounds. Dampen the edges and fold in half to form semi-circular pastries. Seal edges well and crimp to make a frill.

- Arrange pasties on well-greased baking trays. Prick and glaze with egg yolk. Bake in a preheated oven at 180°C (350°F) for 20–25 minutes, or until golden. Serve warm.

miroton of beef

A hearty baked meal of sliced beef and potatoes.

Serves 4

Ingredients

Butter	30 g (1 oz)
Onions	2, large, peeled and chopped
Garlic	1 clove, peeled and minced
Plain (all-purpose) flour	1 tsp
Bay leaf	1
Beef stock	300 ml (10 fl oz / 1¼ cups)
Dry red wine	150 ml (5 fl oz / ⅝ cup)
Salt	to taste
Ground black pepper	to taste
Beef	350 g (12½ oz), thinly sliced
Potatoes	5, boiled, peeled and thinly sliced

Method

- Melt butter over medium heat. Add onions and garlic. Cook for 5 minutes or until onions turn translucent. Stir in flour and reduce heat to low. Add bay leaf.

- Stir in stock and wine. Season with salt and pepper to taste. Bring to the boil and reduce heat to simmer for 15 minutes. Remove from heat and cool.

- Add sliced beef. Return to medium heat and simmer for about 10 minutes.

- Arrange potato slices in a ring around the edge of an ovenproof dish. Arrange sliced beef in the centre. Remove bay leaf from sauce and spoon sauce over beef. Heat under a hot grill for 3 minutes and serve immediately. Garnish as desired.

potato and mushroom bake

This filling potato dish is good enough eaten on its own but for a more substantial meal, serve with grilled bacon, baked beans and crusty bread.

Serves 4

Ingredients

Potatoes	700 g (1½ lb), peeled and halved
Vegetable oil	2 Tbsp
Margarine or butter	55 g (2 oz)
Button mushrooms	100 g (3½ oz), wiped thinly and sliced
Dried mixed herbs	1 tsp (e.g. dried tarragon and oregano)
Salt	to taste
Ground black pepper	to taste
Tomatoes	2, large, thinly sliced

Method

- Cover potatoes with salted water and bring to the boil. Reduce heat and simmer for 5 minutes. Drain and cool.

- Heat oil and half the margarine or butter in a saucepan. Add mushrooms and toss over medium heat for about 3 minutes, until most of the fat has been absorbed. Remove with a slotted spoon.

- Slice potatoes to 0.25-cm (⅛-in) thickness. Arrange half the potatoes in an overlapping pattern in a greased ovenproof dish. Cover with mushrooms and sprinkle with half the mixed herbs. Season with salt and pepper to taste.

- Arrange remaining potato slices in a layer over mushrooms. Finally, top with sliced tomatoes. Sprinkle remaining herbs on top. Melt remaining margarine or butter and pour over dish.

- Bake in a preheated oven at 200°C (400°F) for 15–20 minutes, until potatoes are tender when pierced with a fine skewer. Serve very hot, straight from dish.

potato pizza

This delicious pizza is an excellent dish for dinner, served with a fresh green salad.

Serves 4

Ingredients

Self-raising flour	100 g (3$\frac{1}{2}$ oz)
Salt	to taste
Butter	55 g (2 oz)
Mashed potatoes	250 g (9 oz), chilled
Tomato purée	1 Tbsp
Grated cheddar cheese	1 Tbsp

Topping

Vegetable oil	1 Tbsp
Onion	1, large, peeled and sliced
Red capsicum (bell pepper)	1, pith removed and sliced
Garlic	1 clove, peeled and crushed
Button mushrooms	125 g (4$\frac{1}{2}$ oz), wiped and sliced
Oregano	a pinch
Malt vinegar	2 tsp
Salt	to taste
Ground black pepper	to taste

Method

- To make pizza base, sift flour and salt into a large bowl. Add butter and rub in with fingertips until mixture resembles breadcrumbs. Add mashed potatoes and knead lightly until smooth. Roll out dough and cut into a 25-cm (12$\frac{1}{2}$-in) round, using a large dinner plate as a guide. Refrigerate until ready to use.

- To make topping, heat oil and stir-fry onion, capsicum and garlic gently for 5 minutes or until onion is soft and lightly browned. Remove from heat. Stir in mushrooms, oregano and vinegar. Season with salt and pepper to taste.

- Place pizza base on a greased baking tray. Spread with tomato purée followed by topping. Sprinkle grated cheese on top.

- Bake in a preheated oven at 200°C (400°F) for 15–20 minutes or until base is firm. Sprinkle more grated cheese on top before serving if desired.

NOTE

For a more Italian flavour, top pizza with slices of salami and black olives, then drizzle with a little olive oil to prevent drying out. Mozzarella cheese can be used instead of Cheddar.

bubble and squeak with bacon

A tasty pan-fried mashed potato cake that was traditionally devised to use up leftover mashed potatoes.

Serves 4

Ingredients

Potatoes	1 kg (2 lb 3 oz), cooked, peeled and mashed
Cabbage	450 g (1 lb), cooked and coarsely chopped
Butter	55 g (2 oz), cut into small pieces
Worcestershire sauce	1 tsp
Salt	to taste
Ground black pepper	to taste
Olive oil	60 ml (2 fl oz / 4 Tbsp)
Spanish onion	1, peeled and finely chopped
Lean, streaky bacon	100 g (3½ oz), coarsely chopped
Garlic	2 cloves, peeled and minced
Finely chopped fresh parsley	

Method

- Combine mashed potatoes, cabbage and butter. Season with Worcestershire sauce, salt and pepper to taste. Set aside.

- Heat olive oil in a large frying pan. Sauté onion and bacon until onion is golden brown and bacon, crisp. Stir in minced garlic . Add potato mixture and mix well. Pat into a cake and fry over a steady heat for 4–5 minutes, or until the bottom of cake is brown and crisp.

- Invert potato cake onto a flat plate, then slide back into the pan to cook the other side for another 4–5 minutes. Sprinkle with finely chopped parsley to serve.

glass noodles with potato cubes and minced beef

This tasty mung bean noodle dish coated with a fragrant dark sauce is best served with steamed white rice.

Serves 4

Ingredients

Potatoes	2, peeled, diced and soaked in water
Cooking oil	75 ml ($2^1/_2$ fl oz / 5 Tbsp)
Onion	1, peeled and diced
Minced beef	170 g (6 oz)
Glass noodles (*tanghoon*)	125 g ($4^1/_2$ oz), soaked in warm water to soften and drained
Dark soy sauce	$1^1/_2$ Tbsp, mixed with 60 ml (2 fl oz / 4 Tbsp) water
Beef stock	90 ml (3 fl oz / $^3/_8$ cup)
Sugar	1 tsp
Salt	$^1/_4$ tsp
Ground white pepper	$^1/_2$ tsp

Method

- Drain potatoes and pat dry on absorbent paper to remove excess moisture. Heat oil in a wok over high heat and fry potatoes until golden brown. Remove and drain. Set aside.

- Leave 1 Tbsp oil in wok and stir-fry onion until golden brown. Add minced beef and stir-fry for another 2 minutes. Return fried potatoes to wok and add small handfuls of glass noodles. Mix well.

- Add dark soy sauce mixture and toss thoroughly. Finally, add beef stock, sugar, salt and pepper. Mix well over medium heat until noodles are cooked. Serve hot.

spicy vegetable balti

This colourful vegetable dish is deliciously spicy and full of interesting textures.

Serves 4–6

Ingredients

Balti Sauce

Vegetable oil	2$\frac{1}{2}$ Tbsp
Spanish onions	1$\frac{1}{2}$, large, peeled and chopped
Garlic	2 cloves, peeled and minced
Ginger	2-cm (1-in) knob, peeled and chopped
Fenugreek seeds	$\frac{3}{4}$ tsp
Ground coriander	$\frac{3}{4}$ tsp
Cumin	$\frac{3}{4}$ tsp
Fennel seeds	$\frac{1}{2}$ tsp
Ground turmeric	$\frac{1}{2}$ tsp
Chilli powder	a pinch
Cardamom pods	4
Cinnamon sticks	1–2, small
Vegetable stock or water	200 ml (7 fl oz)
Tomatoes	3, chopped
Bay leaves	2

Vegetables

Spinach	700 g (1$\frac{1}{2}$ lb), leaves and stems separated
Potatoes	2, peeled and cut into small pieces
Ghee or vegetable oil	60 ml (2 fl oz / 4 Tbsp)
Cumin	1 tsp
Fenugreek seeds	1 tsp
Ground turmeric	1 tsp
Garam masala	2 tsp
Chilli powder	$\frac{1}{4}$–$\frac{1}{2}$ tsp
Onion	1, quartered and thinly sliced
Garlic	2 cloves, peeled and crushed
Red capsicum (bell pepper)	1, large, pith removed and cut into 0.5-cm ($\frac{1}{4}$-in) strips
Button mushrooms	450 g (1 lb), wiped and stems discarded
Salt	to taste

Method

- To make Balti sauce, heat oil and stir-fry onions until translucent. Add garlic, ginger and spices. Stir well. Add stock or water, tomatoes and bay leaves. Bring to the boil, then reduce heat. Cover and simmer for 25 minutes, stirring often. Discard cinnamon sticks and bay leaves. Cool slightly and purée in a blender. Set aside.

- Cover and cook spinach over medium heat for 5 minutes or until wilted. Drain well and set aside.

- Boil potatoes in salted water for about 8 minutes or until just tender. Drain well and set aside.

- Heat ghee or oil and stir-fry spices for 30 seconds. Add onion, garlic, capsicum and mushrooms. Stir-fry for another 4–5 minutes. Stir in potatoes, spinach, salt and Balti sauce. Toss gently for 3–4 minutes. Transfer to a serving dish and serve hot.

NOTE

After cooking the spinach and potatoes, ensure that they are well drained or the excess liquid will make the consistency of the finished dish rather thin and watery.

potato casserole

This warm and hearty dish is best served with crusty bread.

Serves 4

Ingredients

Butter	30 g (1 oz)
Shallots	2, peeled and coarsely chopped
Celery	2 stalks, trimmed and coarsely chopped
Garlic	1 clove, peeled and crushed
Potatoes	900 g (2 lb), peeled, halved and thinly sliced
Carrots	240 g (8$\frac{1}{2}$ oz), peeled and thinly sliced
Streaky bacon	4 rashes, chopped
Canned peeled tomatoes	420 g (14 oz)
Chicken stock	250 ml (8 fl oz / 1 cup)
Salt	1 tsp
Ground black pepper	to taste
Paprika	2 tsp
Dried basil	$\frac{1}{4}$ tsp

Method

- Melt butter in a large frying pan over moderate heat. Stir-fry shallots, celery and garlic for 3–4 minutes, or until shallots are soft and translucent. Add potatoes, carrots and bacon. Stir-fry for another 10 minutes until potatoes turn golden brown.

- Pour in tomatoes, including juice from can, chicken stock, salt, pepper, paprika and basil. Bring to the boil over moderate heat, stirring frequently.

- Reduce heat to low. Cover and simmer for 10 minutes or until potatoes are tender. Remove from heat. Turn mixture into a warm serving dish and serve immediately.

mee goreng

This is a mildly spicy and flavourful Indian noodle dish stir-fried with potato cubes.

Serves 4

Ingredients

Cooking oil	125 ml (4 fl oz / ¹/₂ cup)
Firm bean curd	1 piece, diced
Brown onion	1, medium, peeled and diced
Fresh yellow egg noodles	450 g (1 lb), rinsed in warm water and drained
Eggs	2, lightly beaten
Potato	1, boiled, peeled and diced
Green peas	70 g (2¹/₂ oz)
Tomato	1, medium, diced
Green chilli	1, seeded and sliced

Seasoning

Curry powder	¹/₂ tsp
Tomato sauce	2 Tbsp
Chilli sauce	1 Tbsp
Dark soy sauce	1 tsp
Water	2 Tbsp

Method

- Heat oil in a wok and deep-fry bean curd cubes until golden brown. Drain and set aside.

- Leave 2 Tbsp oil in wok and stir-fry onion for 2–3 minutes until soft. Add noodles and seasoning. Mix well and continue to stir-fry over gentle heat for 3–4 minutes.

- Pour in beaten egg and leave to set for 1 minute before stirring to mix well with noodles. Add potato, green peas, tomato and bean curd. Mix well and cook for 30 seconds.

- Transfer to a large serving dish, garnish with sliced green chilli and serve immediately.

For a more tangy flavour, squeeze a lime over the noodles just before serving.

chicken curry with potatoes

This spicy and hearty dish goes well with steamed rice or crusty bread.
Serves 4–6

Ingredients

Chicken	1, about 1.5 kg (3 lb 4$\frac{1}{2}$ oz) cut into large pieces
Onion	1, large, peeled and quartered
Ginger	3-cm (1$\frac{1}{2}$-in) knob, peeled
Garlic	3 cloves, peeled
Red chillies	2
Shallots	55 g (2 oz), peeled
Cooking oil	60 ml (2 fl oz / 4 Tbsp)
Meat curry powder	70 g (2$\frac{1}{2}$ oz), mixed with 100 ml (3$\frac{1}{3}$ fl oz / $\frac{3}{8}$ cup) water to form a paste
Coconut milk	500 ml (16 fl oz / 2 cups)
Water	500 ml (16 fl oz / 2 cups)
Potatoes	3, large, peeled and quartered
Salt	2$\frac{1}{2}$ tsp
Sugar	$\frac{1}{2}$ tsp

Method

- Season chicken with $\frac{1}{2}$ tsp salt and set aside.
- Grind onion, ginger, garlic, red chillies and shallots together finely. Heat oil in a pot and stir-fry ground mixture for 3 minutes. Add curry paste and stir-fry for another 5 minutes until fragrant.
- Add chicken pieces and fry for 5 minutes until well-coated with mixture. Add coconut milk and water. Bring to the boil. Add potatoes, remaining salt and sugar. Reduce heat and simmer for 40 minutes until chicken is tender. Serve hot.

japanese beef curry

A mildly spicy curry with a thick and rich sauce, best served with sticky short-grain rice.

Serves 4

Ingredients

Butter	30 g (1 oz)
Brown onion	1, medium, peeled and finely sliced
Beef	400 g (14 oz), diced
Beef stock	500 ml (16 fl oz / 2 cups)
Bay leaf	1
Carrots	2, peeled and sliced
Potatoes	3, peeled and cut into cubes

Curry gravy

Butter	55 g (2 oz)
Brown onions	2, peeled and minced
Minced garlic	1 tsp
Minced ginger	1 tsp
Plain (all-purpose) flour	2 Tbsp
Meat curry powder	1 Tbsp
Beef stock	375 ml (12 fl oz / 1½ cups)
Garam masala	¼ tsp

Method

- To make curry gravy, heat butter in a frying pan and sauté minced onion for 10 minutes or until slightly brown. Add minced garlic and ginger. Sauté for another 2 minutes. Add flour and curry powder. Sauté over low heat for 1 minute. Gradually pour in stock while stirring constantly. Simmer until sauce is thickened. Stir in garam masala and set aside.

- Heat butter in a pot and sauté sliced onion over medium heat until softened. Add diced beef and sauté until meat changes colour.

- Add stock, bay leaf, carrots and potatoes . Simmer over low heat for 30–40 minutes, or until potatoes and carrots are soft.

- Add curry gravy to beef and vegetable mixture. Simmer over low heat for another 20 minutes, stirring often. Remove bay leaf and serve hot.

simmered potatoes and assorted vegetables

A light Japanese simmered dish to go with steamed rice.

Serves 4

Ingredients

Sugar peas	110 g (4 oz), trimmed
Carrots	110 g (4 oz), peeled and cut into 1-cm ($\frac{1}{2}$-in) slices
Baby potatoes	300 g (10$\frac{1}{2}$ oz), unpeeled, scrubbed and washed
White radish	450 g (1 lb), peeled and cut into 1-cm ($\frac{1}{2}$-in) slices, soaked in cold water
Dashi	7.5 g (1$\frac{1}{2}$ tsp) dashi granules mixed with 750 ml (24 fl oz / 3 cups) water
Sugar	2 Tbsp
Japanese soy sauce	75 ml (2$\frac{1}{2}$ fl oz / 5 Tbsp)
Sake	45 ml (1$\frac{1}{2}$ fl oz / 3 Tbsp)
Mirin	15 ml ($\frac{1}{2}$ fl oz / 1 Tbsp)
Soft bean curd	200 g (7 oz), cut into 4 x 3-cm (2 x 1$\frac{1}{2}$-in) pieces
Button mushrooms	4, caps wiped and stems removed

Method

- Blanch sugar peas in boiling water for 2 minutes, then plunge in cold water. Set aside.

- Add carrots, potatoes and radish to a pot with dashi stock. Bring to the boil, then reduce heat to simmer. Stir in sugar, Japanese soy sauce and sake. Skim off any foam on the surface of stock.

- Cover and simmer for 30 minutes, or until liquid has reduced by half. Add mirin, bean curd and mushrooms. Return to the boil. Finally, add sugar peas and simmer for 2 minutes. Serve hot.

hotpot with chicken and assorted vegetables

A hearty soup dish which is substantial on its own.
Serves 4

Ingredients

Vegetable oil	1 Tbsp
Chicken drumsticks	450 g (1 lb), deboned and cut into bite-size pieces, skin intact
Carrot	1, peeled, halved lengthways and cut into 2.5-cm (1-in) sections
Baby potatoes	300 g (10$\frac{1}{2}$ oz), unpeeled, scrubbed and halved
Celery	2 stalks, cut into 1-cm ($\frac{1}{2}$-in) sections
Canned bamboo shoot	100 g (3$\frac{1}{2}$ oz), drained and cut into 0.5-cm ($\frac{1}{4}$-in) slices
Fresh shitake mushrooms	4, caps wiped and stems removed
Chicken stock	750 ml (24 fl oz / 3 cups)
Light soy sauce	60 ml (2 fl oz / $\frac{1}{4}$ cup)
Ground black Pepper	to taste

Method

- Heat 1 Tbsp oil in a pot and stir-fry chicken pieces until the surface of meat turns white. Add carrot, potatoes, celery, bamboo shoot and mushrooms. Continue to stir-fry for 2 minutes.

- Add chicken stock and bring to the boil. Add soy sauce, reduce heat and simmer for 25 minutes, or until vegetables are soft.

- Add ground black pepper to taste. Serve hot in a large serving bowl.

boiled potatoes and chicken meatballs

A hearty dish which can be cooked at the table in a claypot on a portable stove.

Serves 4

Ingredients

Potatoes	3, medium, peeled, quartered and soaked in cold water
Dashi	10 g (2 tsp) dashi granules dissolved in 1 litre (32 fl oz / 4 cups) water
Assorted fish cakes and fish balls	16
Chicken meatballs	10
Button mushrooms	8, caps wiped and stems removed
Leek	1, large, trimmed and cut diagonally into 1-cm ($^1/_2$-in) slices
Soft bean curd	300 g, cut into 2 x 4-cm (1 x 2-in) pieces

Seasoning

Sake	30 ml (1 fl oz / 2 Tbsp)
Japanese soy sauce	60 ml (2 fl oz / $^1/_4$ cup)

Method

- Place potatoes, dashi and seasoning in a pot. Bring to the boil, reduce heat and simmer for 20 minutes.
- Add fish cakes, fish balls, chicken meatballs, mushrooms and leek. Simmer for another 10–15 minutes. Add soft bean curd. Return to the boil, reduce heat and simmer for 5 minutes. Serve immediately.

chinese-style pork chop and potatoes

A delicious pork chop dish, originally prepared by Hainanese cooks for their British employers.

Serves 4

Ingredients

Pork fillet	300 g (10$\frac{1}{2}$ oz), cut into 4 pieces
Salt	to taste
Ground white pepper	to taste
Sesame oil	$\frac{1}{2}$ tsp
Cooking oil	for deep-frying
Potatoes	2, medium, peeled and cut into wedges
Plain (all-purpose) flour	4 Tbsp, mixed with 1 Tbsp corn flour (cornstarch)
Egg	1, lightly beaten
Dried breadcrumbs	
Butter	30 g (1 oz)
Garlic	2 cloves, peeled and chopped
Brown onion	1, peeled and thinly sliced
Frozen green peas	100 g (3$\frac{1}{2}$ oz), blanched in hot water for 2 minutes

Sauce

Light soy sauce	1 Tbsp
Worcestershire sauce	2$\frac{1}{2}$ Tbsp
Tomato sauce	4 Tbsp
Sugar	1 tsp
Water	170 ml (5 fl oz / $\frac{2}{3}$ cup)
Corn flour (cornstarch)	1 heaped tsp, mixed with 2 tsp water

Method

- Use a meat hammer to tenderise pork fillets. Marinate fillets with salt, pepper and sesame oil. Set aside for 30 minutes.

- Heat oil in a wok and deep-fry potato wedges until golden brown. Drain well and set aside.

- Coat pork fillets in mixed flour, followed by egg and breadcrumbs. Reheat oil in wok and deep-fry pork fillets until golden brown. Drain well and cut into 1.5-cm (3/4-in) strips. Set aside.

- To make sauce, melt butter in a frying pan, then sauté garlic and onion until onion turns translucent. Add peas and sauté for another 2 minutes. Mix ingredients for sauce together except corn flour mixture. Add to frying pan and bring to the boil, then stir in corn flour mixture to thicken sauce.

- Arrange pork fillets and potato wedges on a large serving plate. Pour sauce mixture over and serve hot.

To ascertain the temperature of oil for deep-frying, insert a chopstick into oil. If "bubbles" appear around the chopstick, the temperature is right.

japanese beef and potato stew

A nourishing stew with a slightly sweet flavour. It is commonly served for dinner in Japanese homes.

Serves 4

Ingredients

Cooking oil	1 Tbsp
Beef fillet	250 g (9 oz), thinly sliced
Brown onion	1, large, peeled and thinly sliced
Potatoes	450 g (1 lb), peeled, diced and soaked in water
Water	
Frozen green peas	55 g (2 oz), blanched in hot water for 2 minutes

Seasoning

Japanese soy sauce	60 ml (2 fl oz / $\frac{1}{4}$ cup)
Sake	1 Tbsp
Mirin	1 Tbsp
Sugar	2 Tbsp

Method

- Heat oil in a pot and stir-fry beef and onion for 2–3 minutes. Drain potatoes and add to pot. Mix well and stir-fry for another 2 minutes.

- Pour in just enough water to cover ingredients in pot. Bring to the boil for 2 minutes. Add seasoning, then reduce to medium heat to simmer.

- Skim off any foam on the surface, cover partially and continue to simmer for 20–30 minutes until potatoes are cooked. Add peas and simmer for another 2 minutes. Remove and serve hot.

asian shepherd's pie

A shepherd's pie with an Asian twist. Serve with a fresh green salad on the side.

Serves 4

Ingredients

Potatoes	3, large, peeled and quartered
Butter	55 g (2 oz)
Salt	to taste
Ground black pepper	to taste
Cooking oil	45 ml (1½ fl oz / 3 Tbsp)
Chicken breast	2 pieces, skinned and diced
Garlic	4 cloves, peeled and minced
Minced ginger	1 tsp
Onion	1, peeled and diced
Carrot	1, peeled and diced
Fresh shitake mushrooms	5, caps wiped, stems discarded and sliced
Chopped Chinese chives	3 Tbsp
Chicken stock	125 ml (4 fl oz / ½ cup)

Seasoning

Light soy sauce	30 ml (1 fl oz / 2 Tbsp)
Dark soy sauce	½ Tbsp
Sherry	2 tsp
Ground black pepper	to taste
Corn flour (cornstarch)	1½ tsp with 2 tsp water

Method

* Cover potatoes with water in a large pot and bring to the boil. Reduce heat and simmer for 15–20 minutes, or until cooked and tender. Drain well. Add butter and mash until smooth. Season with salt and pepper to taste.

* Heat 2 Tbsp oil in a frying pan and fry chicken pieces until slightly brown. Remove and set aside.

* Heat remaining oil in frying pan, then sauté garlic, ginger and onion until soft. Add diced carrot, mushrooms and Chinese chives. Sauté for another 3 minutes. Return chicken pieces to frying pan and stir in seasoning except corn flour mixture. Sauté for 1 minute. Add chicken stock and simmer over medium heat for 3 minutes. Stir in corn flour mixture to thicken gravy.

* Spoon chicken mixture into a baking dish and top with mashed potatoes. Make swirling patterns on the surface of pie by pressing lightly with the back of a butter knife.

* Bake in a preheated oven for 25–30 minutes at 200°C (400°F). Remove from oven and place under a grill to brown top if desired. Serve immediately.

glossary

1. Bay leaves

These are dried and brittle leaves of an evergreen tree. Olive green in colour, the leaves are distinctively aromatic and spicy in flavour. Often used in soups, stews, marinades for meats and spice blends such as curry powders.

2. Bean curd

Made from puréed yellow soy beans, bean curd comes in many forms but only two types are used in the recipes here.

Firm bean curd, also known as *taukwa*, is a plain, pressed bean curd, usually available in square shape. Due to its heavy and dense texture, it is highly versatile and commonly featured in dishes that require braising or stir-frying.

Soft bean curd (picture not shown) is smooth and delicate in texture. It is usually sold as a white square or rectangular curd immersed in water. Often used in soup dishes.

3. Cardamom pods

Cardamom pods are from a plant of the ginger family. These pods are greenish brown, or white in colour when bleached in the sun. Possessing lemony undertones, the seeds are usually removed from the pods (15-20 black or brown seeds in a pod) before use. Commonly used in Indian curries and sweets.

4. Cayenne pepper (picture not shown)

A powder ground from dried, ripened pods of a particular variety of red capsicums commonly grown in the West Indies, Central and South America. This capsicum powder ranges from a dark red to orange colour, It is very spicy but has little aroma. It is commonly used in Mexican cuisine where it adds zest to salsa dips and marinades for meats.

5. Cinnamon

These woody, brown-coloured sticks are made from the inner bark of a tropical evergreen tree. They are left to dry in the sun and curl into quills. Warm, sweet and aromatic in flavour, they are blended with other spices for curries and also used in flavouring cakes and breads.

6. Dashi (picture not shown)

A soup stock for Japanese soups and stews made with konbu (seaweed) and dried fish flakes. Nowadays, sachets of dashi granules may be conveniently purchased from Japanese grocery stores or supermarkets which stock Japanese products.

7. Dried / fresh oregano

This herb plant has small, heart-shaped leaves ranging from light to dark green colour and belongs to the mint family. It is available in the dried form, as crumbly green leaves. The herb is strongly aromatic, with minty flavours and a peppery bite. Commonly used to flavour Italian dishes.

8. Dried tarragon

These dried greyish green leaves impart a fresh smelling and sweet flavour similar to anise or liquorice. The herb is known to aid digestion and also acts as an appetite stimulant. Often added to salad dressings and soups.

9. Fresh thyme

This herb plant has small, dark green leaves. It belongs to the mint family and has pungent, earthy flavours, which goes well with stews, fish, stuffings and salads.

10. Fennel bulb

A pale greenish white vegetable with short stems and feathery green leaves, the bulb has a mildly sweet flavour that is similar to anise. Commonly featured in Italian and Provencal cooking. This versatile vegetable can be baked, sautéd, braised or used in salads.

11. Fennel seeds (picture not shown)

These seeds are from the common variety of the fennel plant. Like the fennel bulb, they possess a delicately sweet and aromatic flavour similar to anise or liquorice. These greyish green or yellowish brown seeds with ridges are known to aid digestion. They are blended with other spices to make curry and Chinese five-spice powder.

12. Fenugreek seeds

Extracted from the pods of a bean-like plant, these are small, hard seeds that are yellowish brown in colour and have a pungent, spicy aroma with a slightly bitter aftertaste. An essential component in many Indian curry powder blends.

13. Fromage frais

A soft white curd cheese made from whole or skimmed milk, with the light texture and taste of yogurt. If made from skimmed milk, it is virtually fat-free and a healthy substitute for cream in salad dressings as well as topping for baked potatoes. If unavailable, replace with low fat cream cheese or yoghurt.

8.

9.

10.

12.

13.

14.

14. Garam masala

There are many variations of garam masala. However, the fundamental spices, which make up any garam masala would include coriander, cumin, cardamom and black pepper.

15. Glass noodles *(Tanghoon)* (picture not shown)

Made from mung bean flour, these noodles turn translucent when cooked. They should be soaked in water to soften before use. Often used in soups, stews and salads in Chinese, Vietnamese and Thai cooking.

16. Ground nutmeg (picture not shown)

A powder ground from oval-shaped seeds that are light brown in colour, it has a distinctively sweet and mildly spicy flavour. May be used to flavour breads, cakes and vegetables.

17. Ground cumin

Ground from seeds, this yellowish brown powder imparts a strongly spicy and sweet aroma. It is often added to savoury, spicy mixtures such as curry powder blends and is known to be an appetite stimulant.

18. Ground turmeric

An underground stem that is part of the ginger family, it is ground into a powder. This bright yellow powder adds colour and a pungent aromatic flavour to curry powders.

19. Palm sugar *(Gula Melaka)*

Cylindrical blocks of fragrant, brown-coloured sugar. Made by boiling sap collected from flowering stalks of the palm tree into a thick and concentrated syrup, which is then poured into bamboo moulds to cool and solidify. Used in many desserts as well as savoury dishes in Indonesian and Malay cooking.

20. Dried prawn paste *(Belacan)*

This pungent smelling paste is made from dried prawns which are pounded, and fermented for months before being fried and pressed into blocks. It is widely used in Malay and Nyonya cooking, where it is blended with other spices or seasonings for various spicy dishes such as curries and *sambals*.

21. Split black beans

These lentils are commonly used to prepare Indian foods that require fermentation. They are highly nutritious and easily digestible. The lentils may be boiled, roasted or ground into flour to make Indian pancakes, breads and porridge.

17.

18.

19.

22. Swede

Also known as the rutabaga, this root vegetable with yellowish flesh is widely thought to be a hybrid of the Swedish cabbage and turnip. It is similar but milder and denser, in terms of taste and texture in comparison to the turnip. Often used in mash, stews and casseroles.

23. Tamarind pulp

The tamarind fruit or asam is revered for the acidity and fragrance that it lends to many dishes in Southeast Asian cooking. It is sold in various forms, including whole pods and is pictured here, in the dried pulp form.

24. Mustard seeds (picture not shown)

These seeds are available from two major varieties of the plant which produce either yellowish white seeds, or seeds ranging from black to brown colour. The flavour of the mustard seeds may be described as sharp and hot. When fried in ghee or oil until a "pop" sound is produced, the seeds will taste slightly nutty. They are also often pounded with spices to make Indian curry powders and pastes.

25. Paprika

This bright red and finely textured powder is ground from certain varieties of red capsicums. The flavour of this spice may range from mildly sweet to fiery and pungent, depending on the variety of capsicums used. Often used to flavour dishes in Portuguese and Spanish cuisine.

26. Water convolvulus *(Kangkung)*

A hollow-stemmed vegetable with long, narrow green leaves, commonly found in Asia. The whole plant is edible except for its roots, although younger shoots and leafs are more tender and hence preferred. If unavailable, substitute with spinach.

Weights and Measures

Quantities for this book are given in Metric, Imperial and American (spoon and cup) measures. Standard spoon and cup measurements used are: 1 tsp = 5 ml, 1 Tbsp = 15 ml, 1 cup = 250 ml. All measures are level unless otherwise stated.

Liquid And Volume Measures

Metric	Imperial	American
5 ml	1/6 fl oz	1 teaspoon
10 ml	1/3 fl oz	1 dessertspoon
15 ml	1/2 fl oz	1 tablespoon
60 ml	2 fl oz	1/4 cup (4 tablespoons)
85 ml	2 1/2 fl oz	1/3 cup
90 ml	3 fl oz	3/8 cup (6 tablespoons)
125 ml	4 fl oz	1/2 cup
180 ml	6 fl oz	3/4 cup
250 ml	8 fl oz	1 cup
300 ml	10 fl oz (1/2 pint)	1 1/4 cups
375 ml	12 fl oz	1 1/2 cups
435 ml	14 fl oz	1 3/4 cups
500 ml	16 fl oz	2 cups
625 ml	20 fl oz (1 pint)	2 1/2 cups
750 ml	24 fl oz (1 1/5 pints)	3 cups
1 litre	32 fl oz (1 3/5 pints)	4 cups
1.25 litres	40 fl oz (2 pints)	5 cups
1.5 litres	48 fl oz (2 2/5 pints)	6 cups
2.5 litres	80 fl oz (4 pints)	10 cups

Oven Temperature

	°C	°F	Gas Regulo
Very slow	120	250	1
Slow	150	300	2
Moderately slow	160	325	3
Moderate	180	350	4
Moderately hot	190/200	370/400	5/6
Hot	210/220	410/440	6/7
Very hot	230	450	8
Super hot	250/290	475/550	9/10

Dry Measures

Metric	Imperial
30 grams	1 ounce
45 grams	1 1/2 ounces
55 grams	2 ounces
70 grams	2 1/2 ounces
85 grams	3 ounces
100 grams	3 1/2 ounces
110 grams	4 ounces
125 grams	4 1/2 ounces
140 grams	5 ounces
280 grams	10 ounces
450 grams	16 ounces (1 pound)
500 grams	1 pound, 1 1/2 ounces
700 grams	1 1/2 pounds
800 grams	1 3/4 pounds
1 kilogram	2 pounds, 3 ounces
1.5 kilograms	3 pounds, 4 1/2 ounces
2 kilograms	4 pounds, 6 ounces

Length

Metric	Imperial
0.5 cm	1/4 inch
1 cm	1/2 inch
1.5 cm	3/4 inch
2.5 cm	1 inch

Abbreviation

tsp	teaspoon
Tbsp	tablespoon
g	gram
kg	kilogram
ml	millilitre